BLACK LEGACY PRESS™
WWW.BLACKLEGACYPRESS.ORG

WE BELIEVE IN AFRICA

BY

DR. G.K. OSEI

BLP PUBLISHING
Eastchester New York

For wholesale please visit:
BlackLegacyPress.Org

Available wherever books are sold.
ISBN: 978-1-63652-102-2

WE BELIEVE IN AFRICA

By
DR. G.K. OSEI

CONTENTS

THE LORD IS MY SHEPHERD

PSALM 23

He oppressor is my enemy; I fear him not.He persecuteth me and my brothers, he accuseth me in his courts and sendeth me to jail. He attacks me wherever he findeth me for his own sake. Even though I live among them,

I fear them not for I know all their evil intentions; my blackness, my strength, my boldness shall protect me.

He prepareth a false statement against me in the presence of his people, he annointeth my head with blows and I suffer all the time.

Truly, brothers and sisters, truly accusation and persecution shall follow us all the days of our lives and we shall dwell in his courts and prisons forever unless we fight him.

WE BELIEVE

THE ANCIENTS WHO TELL US THAT THE
AFRICAN PEOPLE ARE LIKE AN INDIA –
RUBBER BALL; THE HARDER YOU DASH IT
TO THE GROUND, THE HIGHER IT WILL
RISE.

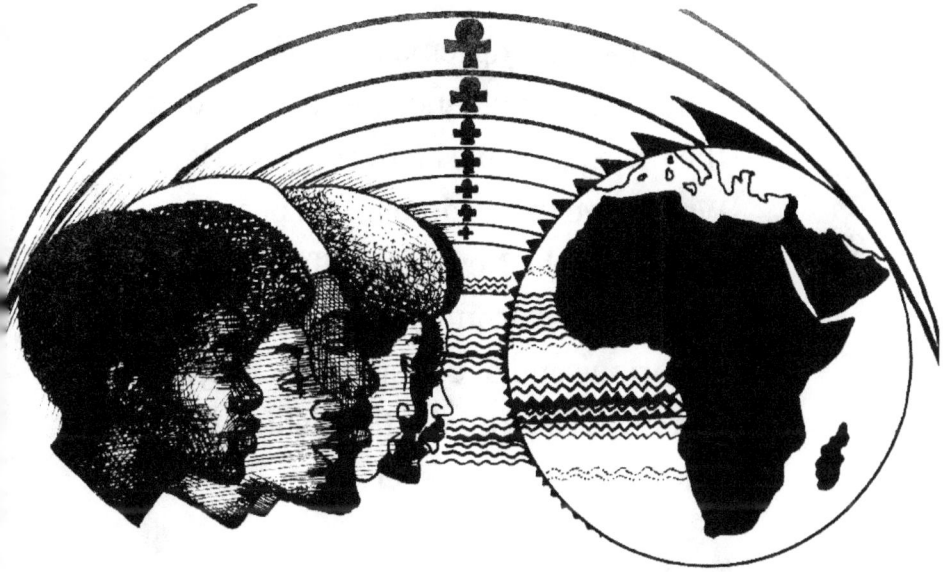

We believe in Africa*

The second largest continent on this planet And in all Black people, its sons and daughters, Who are scattered all over the world, Born true Africans for Africa; Suffering under European domination, We were enslaved, colonized and exploited; We freed ourselves from the yoke of European enslavement And the same day decided to stand together all the time. We ascended into the political kingdom And

sitteth at the supreme head of the African
Empire, From whence we shall protect
the African people all over the world.
We believe in freedom for all peoples,
Especially the New Africa, The destruction
of settler governments in Africa, The
victorious end of our struggle, its glory
and its pride, And the flourishing of
Africa, forever and ever.

* THE AFRICANS' CREED RECALLS THE CHRISTIAN'S.
"I BELIEVE IN GOD"

PSALM 7

◊ Africa my continent, in thee do I put my trust:
save me from all the devils that persecute me,
and deliver me:
Lest he steals my land and my gold, making it
his own, while he enslaves me.

◊ Africa my continent, let not the white men
persecute my body and kill me, let them

perish and their oppressions come to an end.

◊ Arise, Africa, in thine anger, lift up thyself because of the rage of the imperialists: and crush them once and for all.

◊ Let the wickedness of the Europeans come to an end. I will praise Africa because she will protect me from my enemies: and I will sing praises in the name of the Ancestors.

PSALM 5

Give ear to my words, O Lord, consider my meditation.

2 Hearken unto the voice of my cry, my king, and my God: for unto thee will I pray.

3 my voice shalt thou hear in the morning, O Lord; in the morning will I direct my prayer unto thee, and will look up.

12 VERSES

DR. G.K. OSEI

PSALM 5

Give ear to my words, O Africa, consider my meditation.

Hearken unto the voice of my cry, my Africa, and my protector: for unto thee will I pray. The white man shall not live in thy Africa. You shall see to it that they perish. Thou shall destroy the white settlers that are exploiting thy sons and daughters: Africa will persecute all the evildoers.

Lead me, O Africa, in thy righteousness because of mine enemies; make thy way straight before my face.

For there is no faithfulness in their mouth; Their inward part is very wickedness; their throat is an open sepulcher; they flatter with their tongue.

Destroy thou them, O Africa; let them fall by their own counsels; cast them out in the multitude of their transgressions; for they have rebelled against thee.

THE AFRICAN'S PRAYER

European, thou art in Africa Disgrace is thy name;

Thy kingdom go.

Our will be done in Africa

As yours is done in Europe.

We take this day our full freedom
And we shall not be lead into

slavery But will deliver ourselves from exploitation. For Africa is our kingdom, our power, our glorious land. Forever and ever...

Amen.

THE SERMON ON MOUNT KILIMANJARO

Blessed are the sons and daughters of Africa for their land is the richest. Blessed are the strong: for they shall inherit the earth.

Blessed are they that are persecuted in the name of Africa for they shall be heroes of the African Empire.

Blessed are they that are

fighting against the Whiteman's injustices for they shall bring comfort and dignity to all African people.

Blessed are the innocent Africans who are suffering for the crimes they have not committed for their sorrows shall not go unheard.

Blessed are the people who are building Africa for they shall be remembered.

Blessed are they that are fighting the Whiteman's domination all over the world for they shall bring sanity into the whole world.

WE BELIEVE IN AFRICA

DR. G.K. OSEI